Echoes In The Quiet

Poems embracing grief along life's journey

Julia A Hyett

BookLeaf Publishing

India | USA | UK

Copyright © Julia A Hyett

All Rights Reserved.

This book has been self-published with all reasonable efforts taken to make the material error-free by the author. No part of this book shall be used, reproduced in any manner whatsoever without written permission from the author, except in the case of brief quotations embodied in critical articles and reviews.

The Author of this book is solely responsible and liable for its content including but not limited to the views, representations, descriptions, statements, information, opinions, and references ["Content"]. The Content of this book shall not constitute or be construed or deemed to reflect the opinion or expression of the Publisher or Editor. Neither the Publisher nor Editor endorse or approve the Content of this book or guarantee the reliability, accuracy, or completeness of the Content published herein and do not make any representations or warranties of any kind, express or implied, including but not limited to the implied warranties of merchantability, fitness for a particular purpose.

The Publisher and Editor shall not be liable whatsoever...

Made with ❤ on the BookLeaf Publishing Platform

www.bookleafpub.in

www.bookleafpub.com

Dedication

For those who have loved deeply
and lost profoundly,
for the hearts that carry echoes of what was,
and for the souls searching for light
through the shadows of grief—
these words are yours.

And to the one I loved,
whose absence fills these pages,
whose memory shapes every line—
this is for you, always.

Preface

Grief is a language we do not wish to learn,
yet when loss finds us, it becomes a part of our voice.
This collection was born from that voice—
a reflection of the quiet ache,
the raw longing,
and the enduring love that follows loss.
In these poems, I have sought to capture
the journey of a widow's heart:
the heaviness of absence,
the bittersweet beauty of memory,
that grows in the cracks of sorrow.
These pages are not just a testament to grief,
but also to the depth of love that grief reveals.
For to grieve is to have loved,
and to love is to carry that bond beyond time.
This is not a story of despair;
it is a tribute to life, love, and the ways
we continue even when the path feels impossibly quiet.
May these words offer solace, understanding
and a reminder that even in the depths of loss,
we are not alone.

Acknowledgements

For the man who was always my biggest and most passionate fan in literally anything I set out to do, these works and words are for you; My Royboy, my greatest and forever love.
Julia Anne

1. Seasonal Harvest

When in early bloom we were,
New growth of green & blossom.
Our love brought forth in Springtime glow
a family we had chosen.

Warmth of us like firelight
of Summer evening bonfire glow
Sun & moon were witness
to the sparks of passions flow.

Matured and weathered garden
made for years of Fall's fruitful harvests.
Among many other ways
our labors nurtured and sustained us.

Like the aftertaste of a treasured wine
that rests upon my tongue,
Our life of prior seasons made
lay soft upon my soul unsung.

My heart and mind play moments back
each second of each day.
And give me hope to build on
ever since you passed away.

And now it is just Winter's breath
upon my face and nape.
Tingle numb to bitter frost
in silent nights & echoed Faith.

2. Silent Echos

There is a silence I've not known before,
a weight that rests in the corners of our house.
it is not the quiet of peace
or the hush of waiting for something to come.
It is the absence of your breath,
the missing hum of your life played out beside mine.

silence now is heavy with sound;
the creak of the floorboards beneath my steps,
the clock ticks louder than it ever did,
the wind pushing against the windows
as if trying to fill the empty spaces you left.

At night, the bed speaks too.
It groans differently when I lie alone,
its voice a reminder that it once held us both.
I can hear my heartbeat in the dark;
slow and broken, searching for yours.

outside our house the silence too changed;

the rustling leaves do not soothe me-
they only echo the sound of what my life is now missing.
The world around me continues,
but its melody for me is off-key, incomplete.

sometimes, I speak into the quiet,
my voice faltering, unsure of its place.
The silence doesn't answer back but
I feel its presence-
A cold companion ever near.

This is the sound of being without you my love,
a symphony of what remains
when you are gone but your true love's shadow lingers.

3. The Haunting Psalm

Grief is the tide, unbidden, it rolls,
A shadowed current beneath the soul.
At times it whispers, soft as a stream,
a gentle ache in the edge of a dream.

Yet it can surge, a tempest wild.
Drowning the heart, unbridled, defiled.
It pulls you under as you gasp for air,
In its depths is lost what is felt as fair.

some days it pools like a quiet lake,
Still & vast it mirrors heart ache.
You stare at the surface & see your face,
distorted, adrift in its endless embrace.

Grief carves rivers through your core,
Etching paths not seen there before.
It shapes you slowly as waters do,
A vast canyon formed where love once grew.

But like all water it seeks the sea,
A boundless expanse where it longs to be free.
The weight may lessen, the waves may calm,
But griefs' echo lingers, a haunting psalm.

Grief like water cannot be tamed,
A force of nature, unaffected by pain.
It flows through time, it ebbs and crests,
A testament to love, to loss, to rest.

4. Bittersweet Herb

Living without you is a bitter herb,
Sharp on the tongue,
its taste clinging to my every breath.
Grief grows wild around planted seed,
its roots tangled in the soil of my days.

Each moment is steeped in
your absence,
The empty chair,
The hollowed laugh that never reaches its echo.

I swallow the bitterness,
a daily ritual.
A reminder of the feast we once shared.

But even the bitter carries a sweetness-
In the quiet I find you-
The warmth of your voice
Sings within an old melody,
The curve of your smile

in a remembered glance.

Your love remains with me,
a light that refuses to dim.
In every sunrise I feel
the warmth of your hand-
gentle, steady, guiding me forward.

In the laughter of others
your joy whispers.
Reminding me that my life still sings.

Yes, the herb is bitter-
but its sharpness awakens me.
It teaches me to savor all
the sweetness that remains.

The gift of you,
woven into the very fabric
of who I am.

I carry you with me my love,
Not as a weight-
But as a seed planted deep,
it grows still toward the light.
It blossoms as a testament to a love

that even death cannot uproot.

9

5. Fire's Imprint

I remember the warmth of
your hands,
how you held not just my body,
but the shape of my soul.

You touched me as though I were
sacred,
Your fingers tracing the lines
of my being.
Soft, yet certain,
like a sculptor knowing his art.

Desire was never a blaze we feared;
It was a fire we tended together.
Its glow lighting the darkest
corners of our days,
In your kiss I tasted both hunger and home-
a language spoken without words,
only we could understand.

Your passion lived
in the space between us,
in the way your eyes held mine,
like a secret you longed to tell;
in the way your voice softened
when the world fell away
and it was just us;
timeless, infinite.

Now, in this foreign space that
holds your absence,
I feel at times the embrace of our fire.
Not as lost, but a warmth still lingering,
a heat time cannot extinguish,
and that passion remains
etched into the very marrow of my bones

In the stillness of remembrance,
I close my eyes and feel you-
Not gone-
Transformed;
Your love now a steady flame within me.
it warms me,
in this harsh and cold world
I now walk alone, and it lights
the path ahead.

6. The Stillness After

I did not think contentment could find me again,
not here, in the shadow of what was.
But it comes softly,
like the first light of morning,
quiet, unassuming,
warming the edges of my sorrow.

It is not joy—not the kind we shared,
but a gentler companion,
a steadying hand
on the shoulder of my grief.

I find it in the rhythm of small things:
the sun setting without haste,
the scent of rain on the earth,
the sound of leaves whispering to the wind.
These moments ask for nothing,
but give me everything I need.

Contentment does not erase the ache of you—

it holds it tenderly,
makes room for both absence and peace.
It reminds me that life is still here,
unfolding quietly,
offering its simple gifts.

I am not yet whole again,
and in spite of the loss
I am learning to live within it.

7. The Shape of Me

I will not shrink to fit the molds
carved by hands that do not know my name.
I will not smooth the edges of my soul
to appease the world's unspoken rules.
The cracks, the curves, the jagged lines—
they are mine,
and they tell my story.
I am the only one who wears this skin,
walks this path,
carries this light.
To be anyone else
would be to betray the quiet truth
that pulses within me.
There is power in standing bare,
unmasked, unguarded,
letting the world see the colors
that bloom in my heart.
Even when the winds howl
and the rain lashes,
I will not fade.

For authenticity is rebellion—
against the fear of being too much,
against the doubt of being not enough.
It is choosing to show up as I am,
messy and magnificent,
flawed and whole.
I honor myself
by living as the person
only I was born to be.
In this authenticity,
I find freedom.
In this truth,
I find home.

8. Tears Mend Rips in the Soul

They fall, unbidden,
carving paths down the face
like rivers through a barren land.
Saltwater stitching wounds unseen,
washing away the weight of silence.
Each tear a story,
a whisper of what was lost
and what still lingers.
They do not erase the pain,
but soften its edges,
like waves smoothing jagged stones.
In their flow,
grief becomes less heavy,
anger less sharp,
the ache less relentless.
They are the language of release,
the body's way of saying,
I must let this go to carry on.
And when the tears finally dry,

they leave behind a quiet strength,
a fragile yet resilient thread of hope.
The soul begins to mend,
the light returns,
and what once seemed broken
finds its way to being whole again.

9. Fur Baby Kisses

Fur baby kisses are always kind,
a soft nuzzle, a gentle reminder
that love doesn't need words
to speak volumes.
They arrive with wet noses
and wagging tails,
warming the coldest moments,
mending hearts with quiet devotion.
No judgment lingers in their gaze,
only trust, only adoration,
as if you are the world entire
and they were born to love you.
Their kisses heal in ways
human hands cannot—
soothing the ache of loneliness,
melting the sharp edges of sorrow.
In their touch, you remember:
love can be simple,
pure as a paw resting in your hand,

steadfast as the loyalty
in their gentle embrace.

19

10. For Our Daisy Mae

The house feels quieter now,
the echoes softer,
the spaces where you once lay
suddenly too big.
Daisy Mae, my sweet girl,
how do I find the words
for a heart so full of you
now aching in your absence?
Your chocolate coat was the color of warmth,
your eyes pools of endless love.
You knew my every mood,
your tail a metronome of joy,
your kisses a balm
for every heavy day.
I still hear your paws on the floor,
the phantom patter of a love
that followed me everywhere.
I still see you in the corner of my eye,
curled in your favorite spot,
as if you never left.

Grief is the price of love,
they say,
and oh, how I would pay it again
just to hold you once more.
To feel the weight of your trust
pressed against my side,
to call your name
and see your eager face appear.
But I know you run free now,
chasing endless fields of light,
your spirit boundless,
your tail wagging in the winds of eternity.
And though my arms are empty,
my heart carries you still—
always, forever, our Daisy Mae.

11. The Path is Hidden

I stand at the edge of what I know,
peering into shadows that stretch endlessly.
The road before me is quiet,
its twists and turns concealed.
I am small in the vastness,
uncertain, afraid to move.
But You are there,
in the unseen,
in the silence that feels so heavy.
You have walked this path before me,
laid every stone,
charted every step I will take.
You do not give me the map,
only the next step,
the light for my feet
that flickers softly in the dark.
And though my heart strains
to see the end,
I choose to trust the One
who sees it all.

For You have written a story
beyond my understanding,
woven with threads of grace,
even in the places
that feel unraveled.
So I will walk,
not by sight, but by faith,
holding Your hand
through the fog,
trusting that Your plans are good,
even when I cannot see them.
You are my guide,
my strength in the unknown,
and though the way is hidden,
I will follow,
knowing You lead me to wholeness,
to peace,
to You.

12. Stolen by the Thief

How cruel the thief, with hands unseen,
To take the love where life had been.
Cancer crept, a shadowed foe,
And stole the one I cherished so.
You were my heart, my breath, my flame,
Yet now I whisper your dear name.
The world moves on, but I stay still,
A prisoner to this aching will.
Why was your laughter forced to fade,
Your future dreams cruelly unmade?
What justice lies in pain so vast,
In memories clinging to the past?
I rage against the bitter night,
Against a fate that stole your light.
The love we shared deserved much more—
A lifetime, not this fractured shore.
Yet even in my anger's blaze,
I feel your love in softer ways.
A shadowed whisper, a fleeting touch,
A reminder you still love me much.

Though grief and fury share their space,
Your memory softens their cruel embrace.
And while the thief has done its worst,
It cannot claim the love placed first.

13. Your Voice Remains

I hear you in their voices,
not in the words,
but in the way they hold them.
The cadence of care,
the steady rhythm of love
that once filled our days.
When they laugh,
it is not just theirs—
it is yours,
echoing from a place beyond time,
a sound I thought I had lost.
They do not know
how much of you lives in them.
In the way they speak with their hands,
or how their words linger softly,
like the warmth of a fading sun.
I listen and am reminded
that love never leaves completely.
It takes root in others,

growing, changing,
but always familiar.
You are here,
not in the breath of your body,
but in the voices of those
who carry your spirit forward.
Through them,
you still speak.

14. A Reflection of You (Inspired by "Danny's Song")

I see you in him,
not just in the way he stands
or the curve of his smile,
but in the quiet strength he carries,
the kindness that flows
like an unspoken melody.
He walks the path you once did,
steady and sure,
with hands that build
and a heart that heals.
His laugh echoes yours—
a deep, familiar warmth
that fills a room like sunlight.
You were so proud of the man he's become,
how he gives without measure,
loves without fear,
and finds joy in the simplest things.

He carries your wisdom,
not in words,
but in the way he lives.
Sometimes I catch him
looking at the world the way you did—
seeing not just what is,
but what could be.
And I know, even now,
your spirit grows in him,
a seed that became a tree
reaching toward the sky.
Though you are not here to see it to it's end,,
he is your legacy.
A reflection of your best parts,
a continuation of your song.

15. A Canvas of Sorrow's Hue

Grief is a canvas I never chose,
stretched taut beneath the weight of loss.
My artists hand trembles-the brush,
its bristles heavy with the dark hues
of sorrow and longing.
Each stroke feels forced, misplaced, jagged,
an unsteady line cutting across the surface of my current
reality.
Black bleeds into gray,
gray into muted blues,
a palette of pain smeared without form.
The colors do not blend as they should;
they fight, they resist,
a chaos that mirrors the ache in my chest.
No beauty emerges,
only the raw, unfiltered truth
of a heart torn open.
Then somewhere in the act of trying,
a flicker of light, bright contrast to the deep-

a faint trace of gold against the shadows.
A reminder that even in anguish,
a spark remains.
And so I keep painting,
layer upon layer, letting each stroke support the next-
letting the tears fall like water
to soften the edges.
The grief will never be erased,
but over time,
it may become part of a greater picture—
a masterpiece shaped by love,
etched with loss,
and framed in resilience.

16. A Journey like Job's

I stand, like Job, amidst the ruins,
the weight of loss pressing my soul thin.
The winds have stripped my world bare,
leaving echoes where life once bloomed.
I have cried out to heaven,
words raw as stones,
questions sharp and unanswered.
Why must love be taken,
why must grief carve so deep?
Job knew this darkness,
the silence of the unseen,
the aching void where comfort should dwell.
He, too, walked the dust,
his heart a fractured vessel,
his faith trembling but unbroken.
And yet, even in despair,
there was a whisper—
a voice that spoke from the whirlwind,
reminding him of mysteries beyond sight,
of hands that shaped stars

and held the depths.
I am not Job,
but I know his path.
I know the tears,
the cries to a God who feels distant,
the slow unfolding of hope.
For even in this loss,
there is a promise,
a thread of light weaving through the dark.
Though I cannot see the end,
I trust the hand that writes my story,
the same hand that restored Job's joy.
So I walk, step by step,
through the ash and the silence,
holding onto the truth that love remains,
and that one day,
like Job, I will see the fullness of the plan
beyond the veil of my sorrow.

17. For the Brokenhearted

To the hearts weighed down with sorrow,
to those who carry grief like a stone,
there is hope beyond the darkness,
a promise whispered in the depths of pain.
"The Lord is close to the brokenhearted,
and saves those who are crushed in spirit."
(Psalm 34:18)
You are not alone in this valley;
His love walks with you,
a quiet strength holding you steady.
When the night feels endless,
and tears blur the path ahead,
remember His words:
"He will wipe every tear from their eyes.
There will be no more death or mourning or crying or
pain."
(Revelation 21:4)
Your wounds are not too deep for healing,
your pain not too great for redemption.
In the shadow of loss,

His light still shines,
soft, steady, unyielding.
Hold on, even if by a thread,
for He makes all things new.
(Isaiah 43:19)
Through the cracks in your heart,
hope will bloom,
a testament to the love that never ends.
Take heart, dear one,
for this is not the end.
The One who holds the stars
also holds you—
and He will not let you go.

18. A Widow's Heart

A widow's heart is a quiet place,
filled with echoes and shadows,
the weight of love that once was
woven into every beat.
It is a heart that carries two,
hers and the one she lost,
a rhythm altered by absence
but unwilling to let go.
There is a tenderness there,
born of memories too sacred to fade,
of moments that linger in corners
where silence stretches long.
Grief lives here, yes,
but so does gratitude—
for the laughter shared,
for the touch that healed,
for the bond that even death cannot sever.
It is a heart that knows longing,
a yearning to turn back time,
to hold what was and who was,

yet still it beats forward,
a testament to resilience.
In its depths, love endures,
not diminished but transformed,
a light that flickers softly,
guiding her through the shadows.
A widow's heart is a sanctuary,
a place of tears and hope,
of sorrow and strength.
It is the quiet strength of a life rebuilt,
still beating, still loving, still whole.

19. Goodbye Yesteryear

I said goodbye this New Year's Eve,
To the last year of my life I shared with you.
The clock struck midnight, and time moved forward,
While my heart clung fiercely to what we knew.
The fireworks lit the sky with brilliance,
But their beauty felt hollow, distant, cold.
For how can I celebrate what's ahead,
When your hand is no longer mine to hold?
Each passing day feels like a thief,
Stealing the moments we had left behind.
Yet, in the quiet, your love remains,
A constant presence within my mind.
I carry you with me into this new year,
Though the path is lonelier than before.
Your laughter, your warmth, your steady strength—
They guide me through this unfamiliar door.
So as I step into another season,
I do so with tears and gratitude too.
For though I said goodbye to the past we shared,
I will never, ever say goodbye to you.

20. Paris in Color

Sometimes I dream in color of the love
we shared in Paris,
The golden glow of streetlights painting your face,
The Seine whispering its secrets to the night
As we walked hand in hand through cobblestone streets.
Your laughter echoed against ancient walls,
A melody as timeless as the city itself.
The world was vast, yet it shrank to just us,
Two souls caught in the glow of a fleeting forever.
I see you still, in the soft hues of memory—
The crimson of wine on your lips,
The blush of dawn as it touched your smile,
The deep, steady gaze of your hazel eyes meeting mine.
Paris was our canvas, love our brush,
And every moment painted a masterpiece.
Now I wake to find the colors have faded,
Yet in my dreams, they bloom again, vivid and alive.
Sometimes I dream in color of the love
we shared in Paris,
And for a moment, the distance dissolves,

Leaving only the warmth of you,
And the city where we belonged.

40

21. The Train called US

We boarded together,
hands clasped tightly,
as the train pulled away
from the platform of beginnings.
Its steady rhythm carried us forward,
through landscapes unknown,
through seasons that unfolded
like chapters of a story.
We passed fields of golden light,
where laughter spilled
like the whistle's song.
We crossed bridges high above valleys,
pausing to marvel
at the beauty and the depth below.
There were tunnels, too,
long stretches of darkness
where the light seemed far away,
and the wheels groaned
under the weight of it all.
But we held on,

your hand in mine,
steady as the rails beneath us.
Each station brought changes—
some we welcomed with open arms,
others we mourned as the train moved on.
The journey was never still,
yet in every motion,
I found my home in you.
When your stop came,
I could not follow.
The doors closed, and the train surged forward,
carrying me into a future
I did not choose.
Still, I feel you in the hum of the tracks,
in the warmth of the sun through the window.
Your presence lingers in every car,
in the rhythm of the journey we began.
This train does not stop,
and I move forward,
though the seat beside me is empty.
Love, rolls on, it endures.